A Curious Quest for
Absolute Truth

# A Curious Quest for Absolute Truth

## Snippets from the Early Years

## Sharon Mehdi

**Bold Action Publishing**
Jacksonville, Oregon

Bold Action Publishing

*A Curious Quest for Absolute Truth*
Copyright © 2012, 2013, 2017 by Sharon Mehdi
All rights reserved.

ISBN: 9780692973608

Cover Design by Nancy Bardos and Sharon Mehdi

Cover Art by Ellen Anderson

Book Design and Production by
Lucky Valley Press
Jacksonville Oregon
www.luckyvalleypress.com

Printed in the USA

## Also by Sharon Mehdi

*The Great Silent Grandmother Gathering*

*Eleanor Bobbin and the Magical, Merciful, Mighty Art of Kindness*

*The Messages*

# Note to the Reader

This is not a memoir. It is the essence of truth,
distorted by the fallibility of memory,
a fair bit of exaggeration,
some outright fabrication
and a dollop of wishful thinking.
So, come to think of it, maybe it is a memoir.

# Contents

# Preamble

I don't know exactly how old I was the first time I set off to see the world. "Two years, ten months and still in diapers," my mother said every time she told the story. All I know for sure is that one summer naptime I crawled out of my crib, put my favorite doll and a box of Morton's Iodized Salt in my pink cardboard suitcase and toddled off down Olive Street.

George Kerkorian, owner of George's Gas 'n Groceries on the corner of Mission and Delmonte, returned me to my mother. Until the moment she opened the door and saw me dangling under Mr. Kerkorian's hairy arm, she didn't realize I was gone.

"Why would you do such a thing?" she wailed. "Aren't I a good mother? Don't I take care of you? Don't you love me?" I wanted to see what lay beyond Olive Street. Even at two years, ten months I knew love had nothing to do with it.

"Why did she take salt?" my father asked that evening from behind the *Fresno Bee*.

My mother's lower lip quivered. "It was for the cow," she said. "Our baby was going to find a cow so she'd have milk."

My father peered over the paper, first at my mother, then at me. "Not many cows in this part of town," he said.

The next day he bought a roll of screening, some molding strips and a couple of hinges and made a lid for my crib that fastened from the outside. "There," he said, gazing down at a bewildered me through the lid of my crib cage. "Now we won't have to worry."

As it turned out that wasn't true. I was not an unruly child, just curious and determined. I discovered quite quickly that if I hunched over and bounced on my mattress I could pop the screen from its frame with my head, climb through the hole, and be down the street in no time.

"I don't know what I'm going to do with her," my mother sobbed when Mr. Kerkorian and his wife Silvie returned me and my cardboard suitcase the second time that week.

"Maybe she not be your baby," said Silvie who was Armenian and talked funny. "Maybe she try to find real mama."

Had I not looked eerily like my mother, grandmother and great-aunt Lucille, my parents might have welcomed the possibility I was switched at birth. As it was, that night my father installed a hook-and-eye latch to the outside of my bedroom door that he warned he would use *if you ever pull that stunt again!*

The threat of being locked up like Rapunzel in a pink and yellow nursery was enough to curtail my naptime wanderings. It did not, however, dampen my spirit, stifle my curiosity or lessen my desire to explore the neighborhood with a suitcase and a cow. I'd just have to bide my time.

Happily, fate intervened when my father moved the family from central California's prune belt to Berkeley, seat of all wisdom. My mother gave birth to her third child leaving less time to keep track of me. And I started school.

It wasn't long before I came face to face with the puzzlements, perplexities and predicaments that would shape my young life. And one day take me farther from Olive Street than my parents or I ever dreamed.

# Great Big Question Mark

I was six the first time I heard the word immortal, and on its heels, eternal and infinite. Thus were the seeds of obsession sown.

Two years earlier my grandfather had mysteriously disappeared. Mysteriously to me anyway. Everyone else knew exactly where he was—the family plot in Sweet Angels of Mercy Cemetery on Iowa Street.

"When is he coming back?" I asked every few days. The answer was always the same. *With grandpa, you never really know.*

There was something decidedly unsettling about a grandfather who just up and vanishes. What if my grandmother disappeared? What if my parents disappeared? What if *I* disappeared? I had to get to the bottom of it.

"When is he coming back?" I asked my mother for the four-hundredth time. It was the day after my sixth birthday. I guess she thought I was finally old enough to handle the truth, or her own baffling version of it.

She dropped to her knees and looked directly into my eyes. "Grandpa's body is gone," she said with a catch in her voice, "but his soul is immortal."

She spoke the last word with a sort of hushed spookiness. I had no idea what she was talking about.

"When is he coming back?"

My mother moved closer until her face was half an inch from mine, making her look like she had four eyes and no nose. I could smell peanut butter on her breath. "Grandpa's in heaven where he will remain for all eternity." I could feel a little droplet of spit on my cheek as she said eTERnity. I wanted to run. This was obviously not my real mother, but some kind of weird look-alike talking gibberish.

"When is he coming back?"

Her hands gripped my shoulders. Not really a shake, but close to it. "Grandpa's part of the infinite universe," she said with terrifying intensity. "He's everywhere and nowhere."

Well that was just plain too much.

"WHEN IS HE COMING BACK?" I demanded.

My mother let go of my shoulders and stood up, her five-foot-two-inch frame looming over my three-foot self. "Dead," she said. "Grandpa is dead as a damn doornail."

By then my grandfather had been missing from family gatherings for two years. Fact was I didn't even remember what he looked like. So the word dead didn't have the impact it might have earlier. The more immediate problem was all those words that went along with dead.

"What does immortal mean?" I asked my father. Our relationship consisted of questions and answers. Two was generally the limit, the more academic the better. He put the newspaper down and looked at me with a glimmer of pride, this question being an obvious step up from my usual.

"Something that never dies," he said.

"But grandpa died so how can he be immortal?"

"He can't," my father said and picked up his paper indicating

I'd reached my question quota. This wasn't going to be easy.

"What's immortal?" I asked my mother when she tucked me in that night.

"Grandpa's soul is immortal," she said, smiling ever so sweetly. She kissed my forehead and switched off the bedside lamp. Maybe my real mother was back.

"What's a soul?"

"The part of us that never dies." She edged closer to the door. "Now it's time for beddie-bye." My mother said a lot of things like beddie-bye. I was embarrassed for her.

She backed into the hall. "Nighty-night, don't let the bedbugs bite." She closed the door leaving me, the bedbugs and a great big question mark alone in the dark.

# Soul of the Matter

Sunday school never made much sense to me. Mostly we colored Bible story pictures printed in smudgy ditto machine purple on paper we were warned not to sniff. And we sang. Songs like *Jesus loves me this I know, for the Bible tells me so. Little ones to him belong. They are weak but he is strong.*

I had a lot of questions about that song. Did it mean little people belonged to Jesus or only little children? My Auntie Myrtle, for instance, was very short. "No bigger than a minute," Uncle Will always said. Did that mean she belonged to Jesus, but cousin Binny didn't because he had to buy his clothes at Pfenning's Big and Tall? And, if so, how fair was that? The concept was troubling.

I learned early on that asking questions in Sunday school was risky and often resulted in being sent home with a note saying I'd been disrespectful. This, in turn, meant I wasn't allowed to ride my new red Schwinn with balloon tires and push-lever bell.

But soul sounded like a safe Sunday school kind of word. Maybe if I understood it I would understand immortal, which appeared to hold the key to my dead grandfather's fate and perhaps my own.

The only thing standing between me and enlightenment was Mrs. Utley, a large, kindly woman who dabbed her forehead with a wadded-up hankie whenever anyone asked a God question.

"What's a soul?" I asked as soon as she'd passed around the ditto drawings. Out came the hankie.

"A soul?" she said. "Now that's an interesting question. Does anyone know what a soul is?"

All the hands went up amidst a chorus of, "I know! I know!" My face was burning. I had displayed my ignorance to a room full of six-year-olds who were about to mock me.

"Joanie," Mrs. Utley said, "tell Deborah what a soul is." My name is not Deborah, but Mrs. Utley said I looked like a Deborah so that's what she called me.

"It's like Casper the Holy Ghost," Joanie announced proudly. My barely-out-of-kindergarten brain emitted an audible twang.

"I know! I know!" others shouted waving their hands wildly.

Mrs. Utley pointed to Carlene. She and her twin Marlene were the smartest girls in class. When Mrs. Utley was having one of those days she called them Maybelline and Benzedrine and then laughed so hard she had to wipe her eyes and blow her nose.

"It's when you die," Carlene said, "the part that doesn't go in the ground."

"Like your shoes," Marlene added with calm assurance.

"Not your shoes," said Parker Pembry. "Your soul is on your feet, so the grave people have to cut them off."

"Eeeeuuuuuu!" the twins squealed.

"These are all interesting answers," Mrs. Utley said, dabbing her brow with rapid-fire intensity. "But they're not quite right. So I'm going to give you an assignment. When you go home today I want you to ask your parents to explain soul to you."

I groaned. Mrs. Utley dashed off a note that I was sure had the word disrespectful in it.

My last hope was Miss Chesterfield, first-grade teacher at Arlington Elementary. My mother said she'd been a teacher since Hector was a pup. One day I asked if I could see a picture of Hector, but she told me to sit down.

"What's immortal?" I asked.

"What a question from one so young," Miss Chesterfield said. "Come see me when you're older and we'll talk about it."

The whole class snickered. I buried my face in my Dick and Jane reader and vowed to show up on her doorstep the day I turned seven. And I might have, except for one thing. The day before Halloween Miss Chesterfield fell off a ladder and two days later she died.

We were all very sad. The principal told our class what a good teacher she'd been and how much everyone would miss her. And then he said: "May her immortal soul rest eternally in infinite peace." My teeth started to chatter. They kept it up through recess and penmanship.

* * *

"How long does Miss Chesterfield have to stay in heaven?" It was almost dinner time. My mother was spooning fruit cocktail into little glass cups. Hamburger patties sputtered in the Revere Ware skillet.

I still hadn't figured out when I could reasonably expect my grandfather to return. Now there was the question of Miss Chesterfield.

"How long does she have to stay?" I asked again.

"Take these to the table, dear," my mother said, handing me two fruit cocktail cups. I was back in a breath. She gave me two more.

In my family, getting the answer to a question required patience and finesse. I dragged the step stool from the sink to within an inch of where my mother stood at the stove squashing the meat patties with a spatula. I climbed to the third step so my head was exactly even with hers. I put my arm around her shoulder and into her ear I whispered, "How long?"

The last drop of juice from a charred burger skittered across the pan. My mother turned her sweet dimpled face toward me. "For all eternity," she said. "Just like Grandpa."

I could have stopped right there. But, alas, I didn't.

"How many *days*?"

My mother put the spatula down. She wiped her hands on the ruffle of her yellow checked apron, and in a woe-is-me voice that sounded a little like Daffy Duck, said "More. Days. Than. There. Are."

That night I lay on my back in my white spindle bed. I stroked the soft satin edge of the blanket and stared at ceiling shadows cast by my merry-go-round lamp. I thought about my grandfather. I thought about Miss Chesterfield. I squeezed my eyes tight shut and willed myself to understand how dead people who get put in the ground can end up in the sky in a place called heaven where they have to stay for more days than there are. The seeds of obsession were starting to sprout.

A few days later something else was sprouting.

# The Bargain

"Don't scratch!" my mother shouted from the kitchen. I was several rooms away, covered with itchy oozy spots that according to her would leave deeply awful scars if a fingernail ever came in contact with them. So horrible would these scars be that when I grew up no one would marry me. "You'll be an old maid," she said. "You don't want to be an old maid, do you?"

I hadn't thought much about it. Mainly I wanted to scratch. I squiggled my back against the sheet. I rubbed one arm against the other. I pounded the spots on my legs with my fists. Nothing helped.

"Why are you all bumpy?" It was my sister. She was four and wasn't supposed to come near.

"Chicken pops," I said, scrubbing my rib cage with my elbows.

My sister tip-toed across the room until she was inches from me. She surveyed the spots on my face and arms. She pulled the blanket back. She lifted my pajama top. "Where are they?" she asked.

"Where are what?"

"The chickens."

"Your sister's not in there with you, is she?" my mother shouted.

"No!" we yelled back in unison.

A week later I was better, but my sister and brother were covered with spots. A few days after that, so was my mother. My father walked around the house with a blue kerchief tied over his nose and mouth to keep the germs out. He looked like a bandit.

"Do you know how to make coffee?" he asked. I was in first grade. I could barely tie my shoes. "I don't suppose you know how to run the washing machine." I didn't.

That afternoon my father hired Mrs. Bigelow, Practical Nurse. It was the start of The Worst Week of My Life.

Mrs. Bigelow was old and had a mean frowny face. Her hair grew straight up and straight out like somebody had just scared her. She reminded me of the witch in *Hansel and Gretel* and I badly wanted her gone.

"Mind Mrs. Bigelow," my father said the next morning as he headed for the car. I ran after him, but I wasn't fast enough. He climbed in the big black Buick and shut the door.

"Don't leave!" I begged. I jumped on the running board and clung to the edge of the window. "I can learn coffee!"

My father rolled the window up until the ends of my fingers were squeezed purple. I yelped. He lowered the window, backed the car onto the street, and drove off. I sat on the curb sucking my throbbing fingertips until the school bus came.

The first thing Mrs. Bigelow did was rearrange everybody. "I can't be traipsing all over the house with meal trays," she said. She moved my brother's crib from the nursery to the room I shared with my sister. She moved my mother into my bed. When my father got home, Mrs. Bigelow told him he'd have to sleep on a cot in the nursery. The only bed left unoccupied was my parents'. It was big and soft and I loved it. This must mean I got to sleep in it! And I did. With Mrs. Bigelow.

"My mother lets me sleep on the floor," I said that night. It wasn't true, but I was desperate not to sleep with a witch. "Sometimes I get to sleep in the bathtub."

"Well you're not sleeping in the bathtub tonight," she said. "And you'd better not wet the bed, missy. I won't stand for it." I hadn't wet the bed since I was three. That night I wet the bed.

Mrs. Bigelow woke up the instant the first drop hit the mattress. "Stop!" she bellowed. It scared me so badly I kept on peeing.

She jumped out of bed and padded down the hall to the nursery where my father was asleep on the cot. "*You* will have to the change the sheets," she announced.

Shame heaped upon shame as I cowered in the corner watching my father try to make a bed. "No more liquids for her," he said. I wondered if that meant ever for the rest of my life.

\* \* \*

was late getting home from school because Dickie Rubin threw up on the bus. Mrs. Bigelow's face was grim. It was day five of my Worst Week.

"Your sister's in the hospital," she said. My heart started to beat fast. The only people I knew who went to the hospital had babies. Or died! I wasn't clear about how babies were made, but I was pretty sure my sister wasn't having one. Tears rolled down my cheeks and splashed on the black tin lunch pail I clutched to my chest.

"You have no right to cry," Mrs. Bigelow said, wagging her bossy bony finger at me. "*You* are the one who made her sick. *You* gave her The Pox."

In that instant, standing on the green and white linoleum floor in the kitchen of my childhood home, my life changed. My sister was going to die and it was my fault!

I ran out the back door and up the hill to my secret hiding place behind a big rock in the vacant lot next to Mrs. Bonzell's house. I flopped down on a pile of damp stickery leaves and there I made my bargain with God.

"I didn't mean to get my sister sick," I sobbed. "If you make her well, I promise I'll be good." I waited for an answer. None came. "I'll clean my room every day. Cross my heart." God didn't utter a peep. I lay on the ground looking up at the sky through the branches of the live oak tree.

"You can have my two-wheeler," I said. I loved that bike more than anything in the world. I waited. God was silent as the sun.

Finally I took a deep breath. "If you make my sister well," I whispered, "I promise to die when I'm seven." That was the most and best I could come up with. My life for my sister's. It had to be enough. I walked back down the hill, still clutching my black tin lunch pail.

The phone call came two days later. My mother answered upstairs. I picked up the extension downstairs. "I have good news," the doctor said. "Your daughter's better."

"Oh thank God," my mother said in a snuffly voice.

I grabbed the Girl Scout calendar off the wall and ran upstairs. My mother was weeping tears of relief. I waved the calendar in front of her face. "How long till I'm seven?"

"Your sister's not going to die," she said.

"I know. How long till my birthday?"

"Shame on you for thinking about yourself at a time like this," she said with a terrible scowl. "What kind of sister are you?"

That night my father told me I had one Thanksgiving, one Christmas, one Easter and two months of summer before my seventh birthday. I fell to the floor in a shivery shuddery heap of joy. That was practically *forever*. Plenty of time to figure out how I was going to become immortal.

# Fire and Really Bad Stuff

My mother swirled the dishrag back and forth through a pan full of grey water, coaxing a few suds to the surface. From my plate-drying perch on the kitchen stool, I could tell something was wrong. She had the look every child recognizes as trouble.

"This year we're going to visit Grandma Great for Thanksgiving," she said.

Her words, accompanied by an unusually vigorous attack on the meatloaf pan with a Brillo pad, were spoken with measured fierceness: "This (scrub) year (scrub) we're going to visit (scrub scrub scrub)..."

"Who's Grandma Great?" I asked. The name had never come up.

"She's very religious and you'll have to learn a new prayer." That didn't answer my question, but provided startling information nonetheless. The only prayer I knew was "Now I lay me down to sleep."

It was, in fact, the only prayer I thought there was.

"Why do I have to learn a new prayer?"

"Because she'll test you." Test me? My other grandmas didn't test me.

"I don't want to go," I said. I was certain of it.

"You have to. We're all going. Except (scrub) your (scrub) father (scrub scrub)."

More startling news. Why wasn't my father going? My mind somersaulted through a list of possibilities, all dire. "Why isn't daddy going?"

"Let's not open that can of worms," my mother said. The idea that somewhere in the kitchen lurked a can full of worms was enough to divert my attention for the moment.

My mother's family was full of secrets. Her parents divorced when she was five, after which she rarely saw her father. His new wife thought it best that way.

She did, however, spend time each summer with her father's mother—my great-grandmother—a stern, bespectacled

Swedish woman named Inga; a pillar of Pasadena society and a founding member of the Ladies Aid Auxiliary of the Methodist Church. Inga did not drink, smoke, dance, sing, laugh out loud, play cards, go to movies or, so it seems, enjoy herself in any manner whatsoever. During childhood visits, Inga introduced my mother as her niece instead of her granddaughter. "Our little secret," she said.

I, of course, knew none of this because it was, well, a secret.

That night and every night for the next two weeks my mother tried to teach me phrases like hallowed be thy name and forgive us our trespasses, an ordeal made worse by my slight speech impediment.

"Not trethpathes, TRES-PASS-ES."

"I can say trespasses!" my sister chirped.

"Bless your precious little heart," my mother said, giving her an Oreo and a hug.

"Trespasses!" It was my two-year-old brother. My humiliation was complete.

"What's a trethpath anyway?" Would that I could have retrieved the question and squished it back down my throat.

"All the things God must forgive us for if we're going to get into heaven."

"Like what?" I squeaked. I was thinking about the time I dumped the whole box of fish food in the bowl and when the bloated, popeyed guppies died, said my sister did it.

"Like when you're naughty." My fears were confirmed. Heaven had angels and hell had fire and really bad stuff. I was going to hell.

"But that's not all," my mother said. "We must also forgive others' trespasses against us." I was double doomed.

"What if I can't remember everything I did and everything everybody else did?" I said. "Then what? Do I still go to hell even if I try to remember and I can't?" My voice was shrieky shrill. "What if I say 'I'm sorry'? Does God say 'okay'? Does he yell it from heaven?" I yelled. "There's probably people saying 'sorry' all the time so they won't go to hell. Is God yelling 'okay' all the time? Is he? Because I've never heard it. Not even once!"

"Make her stop," my sister whimpered.

"So how do I know he heard the 'sorry' if I can't hear the 'okay'? Besides..."

My mother shoved an Oreo in my mouth.

By the time we got to Pasadena for Thanksgiving, I was a stuttering, cookie-addicted, hell-bound wreck. And it was about to get worse.

"Remember," my mother said as she pulled our suitcases up the front steps of Grandma Great's house, "Christmas is just around the corner. Santa sees and hears everything."

That was the final straw. Hell, Grandma Great, and now Santa Claus.

I'd been confused about God and Santa for a long time. There seemed to be a lot of overlap. God saw everything. So did Santa. They both rewarded the good and punished the bad. Well, God punished and Santa withheld Sparkle Plenty dolls.

Both had long white beards and lived in the sky. And both were used by my parents to control behavior:

"If you don't eat your Brussels sprouts (liver loaf, parsnips, cauliflower), Santa won't bring you any presents."

"You know what God does to children who tell fibs." I didn't know, but it was bound to be enormously awful.

Of the two, Santa seemed the more approachable. Last year I'd seen him at Hink's, Capwell's and The Emporium. I'd heard rumors he wasn't real, but decided to ignore them. Maybe I could tell Santa I was sorry for all the trespasses and he could say "okay" and it would be enough to satisfy the new scary grandma and keep me out of a fiery pit. I did not dare hope for more, like a doll for my very last Christmas.

In my family we didn't say grace before meals, even on Thanksgiving. So when my mother warned with her most threatening look and a tug on my earlobe for emphasis: "Don't you dare begin eating until Grandma Great says grace." I thought grace was a word she would say. I didn't know it was a prayer. The longest prayer I had ever heard. A prayer that made me fidget and squirm and feel like I was going to burst into high hysteria.

When Grandma Great finally said, "Amen," I was weak from the strain and starving.

My mother put turkey on my plate and stuffing and cranberry sauce and sweet potatoes covered in marshmallows. My favorites! I looked around the table. Everybody was eating. All the cousins, the aunts and uncles, my sister, my mother, even Grandma Great took a bite of turkey.

"When's she going to say grace?" I whispered.

"It's not polite to whisper, young lady," Grandma Great said. "Why aren't you eating?"

I nudged my mother. "Grace," I said under my breath, trying not to move my lips. She answered my pleading look with one of her own.

I was a child with a deep need to please. And a deeper need to avoid punishment. I picked up a fork full of marshmallow-laden sweet potatoes and raised it, millimeter by painfully slow milli-meter, hoping beyond hope that Grandma Great said the word grace before the food got to my mouth.

"What's the matter with her?" Grandma Great asked my mother.

"What's the matter with you?" my mother asked me. I felt wild panicky laughter starting to rise from my toes. Everybody was looking at me.

"Speak up, girl!" Grandma Great said.

"Stop playing with your food!" my mother said.

It was hopeless. No matter what I did, somebody was going to smack me.

In one desperate instant that I knew I would remember for the rest of my short life, I simultaneously shoved the fork in my mouth, screamed, "Say grace!" and exploded into a burst of hyena laughter that sent sticky sweet-potato goo flying all over the table.

That night, after Grandma Great soaked the tablecloth in Oxydol and padlocked the leftovers in the big Philco refrigerator, she sat in a chair by the bed as I, a quivering jittering mess of a child with tears of terror running down my face, knelt to say the prayer on which I would be tested.

"Dear Santa, I'm sorry about the sweet potatoes and the guppies and the trethpathes and giving my sister chicken pops, and if you're not God, tell him what I said, but if you can say 'okay,' please say it now, and if you can't, tell God to say it loud enough so I can hear and Grandma Great can too, and please, please tell me how to be immortal. Amen."

The room was so quiet I could hear my heart beating in my ears. I was afraid to look up. I was afraid to breathe. Finally, in a mighty voice with only a hint of Swedish accent, I heard the words that, for the moment, set my worrisome complex world aright.

"Good enough," she said. "Good enough."

# Who Wants to Play the Virgin?

"Who wants to play the Virgin?" Mrs. Utley asked. The first and second graders were putting on a Christmas play.

"I do! I do!" Gordon Phinney shouted. Carlene and Marlene whooped and flounced in their seats.

"You can't play the Virgin, you're a boy," said Carlene.

"You're a boy," Marlene echoed.

"What's a virgin?" I asked. Until that very moment I thought Virgin was Mary's first name.

Mrs. Utley fumbled in her pocket for the hankie wad. She leaned over and whispered in my ear. "Jesus' mother was a virgin." Beads of sweat were starting to collect at her brow line.

"But what is it?" I whispered back.

The sweat was now running down Mrs. Utley's cheeks and dropping from her chin onto her shiny green blouse. All the hankie dabbing in the world couldn't stem the flow. The class watched transfixed.

"Someone who never did it," Carlene said flouncing a double flounce.

"Did what?" said Gordon Phinney.

Before I had a chance to say, "Yeah, did what?" Mrs. Utley grabbed a fistful of ditto drawings and flung them at us. "Let's see who can color the fastest!" she said, shooting a wooden box full of stubby Crayon pieces down the table. "Quick! The winner gets a Lifesaver!"

"Mrs. Utley won't let Gordon Phinney be the virgin because he's a boy," I said when my father picked me up from Sunday school. I was sitting in the back seat of the big black Buick. I could see his eyes in the rearview mirror. They were popped wide open.

"What's a virgin?" I asked.

He cleared his throat so many times it sounded like the night he got a fish bone stuck. "That's a question for your mother," he said. My mother answered questions about schoolwork, chores, when I had to be home, and where babies come from.

I hoped with all my heart that virgin didn't have anything to do with where babies come from.

"Remember when we talked about where babies come from?" my mother said. She was heating Spam in the frying pan.

Oh please no.

"Jesus' mommy and daddy didn't make a baby that way so his mommy was a virgin."

Well that answered nothing. I could think of a dozen questions, but I was afraid my mother would start telling me about how daddy put his hotdog in mommy's donut and made a baby. I was the only six-year-old, probably in the world, who wouldn't eat hotdogs or donuts because I thought they might be sort of like relatives.

"Here's the list," Mrs. Utley said the following week. "Joanie, you'll be Mary. Gordon will be Joseph. Carlene and Marlene will be angels. Billy, Alexander and Tobias, you'll be the Three Wise Men, and Deborah (that was me), you'll be the Star of Bethlehem."

"I'm going to be the star in the Christmas play," I said when my father picked me up from Sunday school.

"The star? Well my goodness," he said. "Congratulations. I'm proud of you." I couldn't remember my father ever saying he was proud of me. I could see his eyes in the rearview mirror. They were crinkling at the edges. He was smiling. He hardly ever smiled. "Who knows, maybe we'll see your name up in lights one day." My father ran movie theaters. When I was born he put my name and my weight on the marquee of the Kinema Cinema and had a photographer from the newspaper take a picture of it. My mother glued it in my baby book along with the cancelled check for $142 from Dr. Perquatty's Maternity Hospital where I was born.

"Guess what!" I plunked the Baby Jesus ditto drawing on the kitchen table.

"I'll be finished in a minute." My mother was making deviled-egg sandwiches. It was precision work. Five pieces of

Langendorf White Bread lined up exactly even on wax paper; five scoops of chopped egg; five iceberg lettuce leaves; five Langendorf toppers. Then the cut. Straight across if it was family. Diagonal if we had company.

She dropped the knife in the dishpan. "What dear?"

If my father was proud I was going to be a star, my mother would probably dance around the kitchen. I was giddy with anticipation. "I'm going to be the Star of Bethlehem in the Christmas play!"

"The Star of Bethlehem?" Her smile faded. She wiped her hands on her apron and pulled my face toward her in a suffocating head hug. "That's too bad, dear. I know you must be disappointed." Life was confusing.

My father didn't come to the Christmas play. Maybe because I was going to be the Star of Bethlehem instead of The Star. Or maybe just because he didn't like churches. I stood on a chair holding a big cardboard star covered in tinfoil. My one line was: "I light their way." I practiced it a thousand times. When it was my turn to speak, I said loudly and clearly: "I white their lay." My mother said nobody noticed, but I knew it wasn't true because a lot of people laughed.

That night my father hammered a wooden stand to the trunk of the fir tree that had been sitting for a week on the front porch in a bucket of water. "It's crooked, dear," my mother said when he positioned the tree in front of the living room window.

"Looks fine to me," he said. "What do you think, girls?" He never asked me or my sister what we thought. The tree was lopsided and listing, but we agreed it looked fine. We wanted to get on with the decorating.

My father wrapped the tree in fat colored lights; my mother hung ornaments; my sister and I threw matted globs of silvery tinsel on the branches. When we were done we stood back and admired our creation.

It was a perfect family moment. Until my sister asked if Jesus had a Christmas tree. "Christmas trees don't have the first thing to do with Jesus," my father said, "and neither do Santa Claus or elves or reindeer or toys. Macy's Department Store made it all up, and if you're smart you'll take a good hard look at just how un-Christian Christmas really is." Then he started in on the Easter bunny.

My sister and I cried. My mother stamped her foot over and over, which was the maddest we'd ever seen her. My father, who was very good at changing the subject, said we could all open one present.

Mine was a doll. My father suggested I name her Inga.

Two days after Christmas the postman delivered an envelope addressed to me. It had purple flowers around the edge. I ripped it open. Inside was a note written in cursive. I handed it to my mother.

"It's from Grandma Great," she said.

Uh-oh, that couldn't be good. Maybe she'd changed her mind and I hadn't passed the prayer test after all.

"What an odd message." My mother turned the note over.

"She's getting old, you know."

"What does it say?" I held my breath.

"I'm afraid it doesn't make much sense."

"But what does it say?"

"I hardly know what to make of it."

"WHAT DOES IT SAY?"

"Well, it says, *Write one book filled with absolute truth and it will make you immortal.*"

I couldn't believe my ears. Did Grandma Great say immortal? "Read it again!" I shouted. My mother read it again. She did say immortal! I grabbed the note and hugged it to my chest. I twirled till I was dizzy. I kissed my mother's cheek a hundred times.

"How long till my birthday?"

"Eight months, dear."

"How many weeks?" My mother looked at the ceiling. She always looked at the ceiling when she was counting in her head.

"About 32."

All I had to do was figure out absolute truth and write a book before my birthday and I'd be immortal! And I had 32 whole weeks!

"How long does it take to write a book?" I asked Miss Bowen during recess. Our new teacher was pretty with hair that bounced when she walked. She wore fuzzy sweaters.

"Oh my, that can take a long time."

"How long to write a short book?"

"That depends," she said. "Do you want to write a book when you grow up?"

"No, I want to write one now so I can be immortal and I won't have to die on my birthday because I made my sister sick."

Miss Bowen stopped and knelt down even though she had playground duty and two boys were fighting over the kickball. "And what do you want to write a book about?" she said.

"Absolute truth."

That afternoon she gave me a note to take home to my parents. When I asked if I'd been disrespectful, she said no and hugged me.

Right before the bell rang, Miss Bowen asked if we had any questions. I raised my hand.

"What's a virgin?" She added a P.S. to the note. My parents wouldn't tell me what it said.

# Two Cloves and a Sticky Spot

Pets had a way of disappearing at our house. Abruptly and permanently. I'd wave goodbye in the morning to a dog or a parakeet or a hamster, and by the time I got home from school it was gone. "Tippie went to live on a farm in the country where he'll have lots of other animals to play with," my mother said. Tippie was a collie with a lump on his stomach that my mother had to rub with cocoa butter.

"Can we visit him? Can we go now? Can we?" I had never seen a farm, or the country for that matter. The prospect was exciting.

"I think we'd better let him get used to his new surroundings before we visit." And that was that for Tippie.

Gregory and Mary Ann were the goldfish I won at the Colusa County Fair. According to my father, the fish decided right after I left for school one morning that they wanted to swim in the ocean with the other fish.

"That's not true! Goldfish can't tell you what they want!" My father lowered his newspaper just enough so I could see his eyes.

"Telepathy." He uttered this strange new word with such certitude I didn't even ask what it meant.

The hamster I inherited from Deanie Landis when his mother became allergic to hamster hair lasted a week. In the morning he was in his cage munching carrot tops. When I got home the cage was empty. "He must have squeezed through the bars," my father said.

"He's too big to squeeze through the bars!"

"Then maybe Mrs. Crumley flattened him." Mrs. Crumley was our ironing lady. She was short and fat and wore cotton stockings rolled at her knees. Every time she bent over I could see her long baggy pink underpants. It was a terrible sight and I didn't want to look but I couldn't help myself. If I went in the kitchen while she was ironing she'd spit on the iron and yell, "Go away or I'll flatten you!"

I, like most six-year-olds, wanted desperately to believe everything my parents said was true. The world and my small place in it was safer that way. So against all reasoning, I decided to believe my father was right. Mrs. Crumley took the hamster out of his cage, ironed him flat and put him back, and that's how he got through the bars. Never mind that it made no sense on any level.

I looked everywhere a flat hamster might hide, but I never found him.

My favorite pet was a cat named Sandy. He was big and orange and mean. I was the only one he didn't hiss at so he became mine by default. During the day he slept in a cardboard box on the back porch. If my father came too close when he took the garbage out, the cat would puff up like a porcupine and growl and yowl and hiss, and my father would run back in the house yelling, "DO something about that cat!"

Mr. and Mrs. Dudley lived next door. Mr. Dudley was a professor at the university and Mrs. Dudley sang high screechy songs my mother said was opera. The Dudleys didn't like kids and they didn't like cats. I didn't like opera.

Mrs. Dudley invited a lot of people to their house for dinner the Easter I was six. She cooked a ham covered in pineapple rings and cloves and canned cherries mixed sticky with brown sugar. I know this because Mr. Dudley didn't close their basement door all the way and Sandy snuck up their back stairs to the kitchen and pulled the ham off the counter where it was cooling and dragged it down the stairs and out the basement door and across the yard to our back porch while Mrs. Dudley was singing for their company.

"Your cat stole our ham!" Mr. Dudley was standing at our front door and his face was splotchy red. "We have eight guests for dinner and your cat stole our ham!"

My father said he was sure the cat couldn't possibly have done such a thing. "I followed the trail," Mr. Dudley said. "The cat is on your back porch right now eating our ham. What do you propose to do about it?"

My father took out his wallet. He removed the thick rubber band that he said protected it from pickpockets and gave Mr. Dudley all the money he had, which looked like a lot to me. Then, because Sandy was my cat and I was responsible for every bad thing he did, my father twisted my ear until I squealed.

When I got home from school the next day Sandy and his food dish and his cardboard box and the ham were gone from the back porch. All that was left were two cloves and a sticky spot.

"Where's the cat?" I asked my mother.

She was mopping the kitchen floor and didn't look up. "You know Sandy," she said, "could be anywhere."

"Where's his food dish?"

My mother stopped mopping. Her eyes got very big. "Hmm. Fooood dish," she repeated, like it was the first time she'd ever heard those words. She looked in the oven. "Fooood dish…" She opened the refrigerator. "Hmm. Where could it be?" I was getting scared.

She stood on her tiptoes and opened the cupboard above the sink, the one I couldn't reach even with a chair. "Well, well, look what we have here." I expected it to be the fooood dish. Instead she pulled down a box of chocolate-covered marshmallow cookies she'd hidden behind the stack of Campbell's soup cans.

"I don't want a cookie, I want my cat!" I ran out the back door and up the street calling for Sandy. I knocked on all the neighbors' doors—all except the Dudleys. No one had seen him.

That night when my father came home for dinner his hands and arms were covered with scratches and Mercurochrome. He had a Band-aid on his neck and a little rip in his trousers that my mother thought she could mend. When I asked what happened, my father said he'd had a run-in with a tiger.

"There aren't any tigers in Berkeley!" I didn't know that for sure, but I hoped it was true.

"Eat your meatloaf," he said. "Your mother worked her fingers to the bone to prepare this meal." I looked at my mother's fingers. There were no bones showing.

The day before school let out for the summer Miss Bowen read our class a chapter from *Animals of the Wild*. She asked if anyone had ever seen a wild animal. I raised my hand. "My father got all scratched up by a tiger."

"My goodness," she said, "that's hard to believe."

"I know," I said. Fact was, in my family there were a lot of things that were hard to believe which did not bode well for my attempt to pin down absolute truth by August.

# No Such Word

"Don't ever let me hear you say you can't do something," my father said. "There's no such word as can't." He was trying to teach me how to throw a ball. The best I could do with deep determination and monumental effort, was lob it in the air and watch it spiral to the ground two feet in front of me. "You're throwing down not out. Throw out!"

"I can't," I wailed. And that was the terrible truth. I couldn't throw balls or kick them or hit them with a paddle or a racquet or a bat. I couldn't get them through a hoop or over a net or in a hole. And worst of all, I couldn't catch them. If a ball looked like it was heading my way I turned my back, hunched down and covered my head.

Since everything we did at recess had something to do with a ball, I lived with daily humiliation. Which is how I ended up in Craigmont Park with my father one early summer morning.

"There's nothing you can't do," he said. That wasn't true. I couldn't lift a building. I couldn't grow as tall as a giraffe. I couldn't count all the grains of sand on all the beaches in the world in one second.

"You could if you set your mind to it," he said. This kind of thing made me crazy. How was I ever going to figure out absolute truth if I couldn't believe my own father?

I decided to put his theory to the test.

That night I lined up my three favorite dolls at the foot of my bed. I plunked myself cross-legged in the middle of the mattress facing them. I closed my eyes and concentrated as hard as I could. I wrinkled my brow for emphasis. "Okay," I said with fierce resolve, "turn into real babies!" I opened my eyes. They were still dolls.

I decided to give it one more try. This time I concentrated so long my head started to hurt. "Turn into babies!" I commanded, and for good measure added, "Abracadabra!"

Even though I was sure it hadn't worked there was, I have to say, a second of breath-catching expectation before I opened my eyes. A flash in time, one tiny instant when I almost *almost* believed it was possible.

That summer my father gave me three choices. I could take tennis lessons, I could take golf lessons or I could learn to swim. I chose the one without a ball.

The extent of my water skills was taking a bath, running through the sprinklers and wading up to my belly button in Lake Anza. But how hard could swimming be? You flap your arms and kick your legs. I could do that.

My mother signed me up for the beginners' class at Berkeley Women's City Club. She bought me a one-piece swimsuit sheared all over with elastic thread that my sister and I quickly discovered we could both fit into at the same time. The print was Hawaiian—orange background with bright pink hibiscus and a green and yellow parrot. A white rubber bathing cap that came down to my eyebrows and fastened with a chin strap, a pair of goggles and a blue nose plug completed the ensemble.

"Oh dear goodness," my mother said when I came out of the City Club dressing room.

She swaddled me tight as a tourniquet in a black and white striped beach towel. "I'll be right there in the stands the whole time," she said. "Don't worry, I won't let you drown." If that was supposed to be reassuring, it didn't work.

It had not occurred to me that there would be boys in the class. Especially boys I knew. Especially *especially* Fred Pitzer and Petey Soderstrom, the two cutest boys in the whole school.

"Let me help you, dear," the swimming teacher said as I wriggled toward her. She freed me from my striped encasement and pointed me in the direction of Fred and Petey who had stopped splashing and were now gawking at me.

It was a short walk to the side of the pool, but all of a sudden I was desperately aware that my feet splayed outward. Since kindergarten I'd had to wear ugly brown oxfords that the man in the shoe store said would correct my duck walk, but so far the shoes hadn't helped and my father still quacked occasionally when he saw me coming.

Fred and Petey watched as the vision that was me in my Jane of the Jungle swimsuit, bathing cap, goggles and nose plug walked purposely pigeon-toed to the edge of the pool.

By the end of week two, I'd discovered there was more to swimming than flapping my arms and kicking my legs. The flapping and kicking, it turned out, had to be done more or less simultaneously. I could flap. Or I could kick. But I couldn't flap *and* kick. And I certainly couldn't flap and kick while my face was in the water.

What I could do was float. I loved floating. On my stomach, bobbing gently on the surface of the water, completely limp, with my arms and legs dangling. I could hold my breath a long time. I could hold my breath so long, in fact, that one morning my terrified mother tore out of the stands screaming, "Save her! She's drowning!" Which I didn't hear because my face was in the water and I was wearing earplugs under my bathing cap. So it came as quite a surprise when my mother showed up fully dressed—silk suit, pearls and patent leather pumps—in the Berkeley Women's City Club pool to save me from floating.

Fred Pitzer and Petey Soderstrom saw the whole thing.

# Does God Remember Promises?

Every Saturday, for the admission price of two 7-Up bottle caps, kids under 12 could watch hours of cartoons and serial episodes of *The Lone Ranger* and *Hopalong Cassidy* at my father's theater on Shattuck Avenue. My job before the show and during both intermissions was to guard the entrance to a wide and winding staircase that led to the balcony. This I did by standing behind a thick red velvet rope strung between two brass poles with my arms outstretched.

"I don't want any hoodlums or hooligans getting past you," my father said. I was not quite seven. I had never seen a hoodlum or a hooligan, but I lived in fear that one would turn up. My father's belief was that every 11-year-old boy in the theater was waiting for the chance to sneak past me, dash to the balcony railing and pelt the children below with Jujubes and Black Crows. The boys would then, in the process of horsing around, fall over the balcony and crash onto the heads of kindergarteners. Children would die, my father would go to jail, my mother would go to the poor house, and I and my siblings would have to live in Bakersfield with Auntie Glenn and Uncle Bill.

Mine was a heavy responsibility. Lives were at stake. My father paid me twenty-five cents a week and didn't allow me to leave my post even to go to the bathroom.

When my mother suggested I might like a theater party for my seventh birthday and added that as a special treat we could all sit in the balcony, I was so excited I bounced around the house like a beach ball.

My mother loved movies and movie stars. She bought magazines like *Photoplay* and *Modern Screen* and read me stories about June Allyson and Margaret O'Brien. Once my father brought a movie star home to dinner. His name was Forrest Tucker which was the funniest name I'd ever heard. My mother wore her best party dress that night and sparkly earrings and sprayed herself with so much Chantilly we had to open the dining room windows. Every time Forrest Tucker said a word she grabbed his arm and laughed a deep gurglie kind of laugh that terrified us all. I begged to be excused from the table even before dessert.

I hadn't thought much about my bargain with God since school let out for the summer. Once in a while, after my mother tucked me in and turned off the light, I'd try to imagine myself dead. I could see me with wings flying around from cloud to cloud, but I still didn't understand how I'd get from a box in the ground to the sky, and no one would tell me.

"How long do I have to stay in the box?" I asked my father. "What if I have to go to the bathroom? Who makes me dinner? Is there a flashlight? When can I come home? Can I call you on the phone?" He started to blink very fast.

"Mother! She's doing it again!" he yelled. He always called my mother "Mother."

"Just please TELL me," I begged.

He wouldn't or couldn't, and eventually I stopped asking.

"What if you promise God something and then you don't want to do it?" It was one week before my birthday. My mother was hemming my sister's blue pinafore. I plopped myself down on the couch next to her.

"Well now, that wouldn't be good, would it?" she said.

"But what if you want to do something else instead?" I was thinking, of course, about writing a book that would make me immortal. "Would God make you do the first thing anyway?" My mother pushed the needle through the fabric with a thimbled finger.

"God doesn't make us do things, but there are consequences." I was afraid to ask what consequences meant.

I took a quavery breath. "I know a girl who promised God she'd die if he did something she wanted him to do, and he did it and now she doesn't want to die."

My mother put down her sewing. She took an embroidered hankie from her pocket, wet the corner with her tongue, and wiped strawberry jam from my cheek. She ran her hands over my hair and straightened my barrette. She looked deeply into my eyes. "Did you put the jam away?"

"Look what mommy gave me for your birthday!" My sister was holding a bubble blower and a coloring book. My mother gave us all presents when one of us had a birthday. She didn't want anyone to feel left out. It was August 23rd, the day I turned seven. I was sitting at the kitchen table trying to write a book filled with Absolute Truth.

So far, I had: "When a thing is true it is true. Like rain or being fat." I wanted to write hungry instead of fat, but I didn't know how to spell it. If I put one word really big on each page and drew a picture of rain and one of Dickie Rubin who was very fat, and put my first name and middle name and last name on three separate pages, that would make 17, which was almost as many pages as my *Mac and Muff* reader.

"I need something to hold my book together." I had just put the finishing touches on Dickie Rubin. My mother gave me a safety pin.

"I made a book," I said to the little bit of blue sky I could see between the branches of the live oak tree. I was out of breath and lying on the ground behind the big rock in the vacant lot next to Mrs. Bonzell's house. "Here," I said, thrusting my 17 pages skyward. "Do I still have to die?" God didn't answer. He never did.

I picked the prickly oak leaves off my socks and laid some twigs on the book so it wouldn't blow away.

At five minutes to noon I was still alive and standing in front of the United California Theater with Joanie Hooper, Harriet Bean, Andrea Sommers and Jackie Barnhill. Jackie was a boy and I loved him. We sat in the loges in maroon velvet seats with head rests. My father gave everyone popcorn in crinkly red-and-white striped bags, the kind of bags he said hoodlums and hooligans blow into like a balloon and slam-pop with their hand. He warned us not to do that.

We saw *Bambi*. I cried and so did my mother and so did Jackie Barnhill. Afterwards we all squeezed into the back seat of the big black Buick and headed home for cake and ice cream. Everyone shouted at once about their favorite part of the movie while I cupped my hands over my mouth and pleaded a whispered plea. "If I have to die please, please, please don't make me do it till after the presents."

Andrea was the last to leave. As soon as her mother's car pulled away from the curb, I ran up the street to see what God had to say about my book. I wasn't dead so he must have liked it. Maybe he'd put a gold star in the corner like Miss Bowen sometimes did. Or wrote "Good work!" in blue pencil.

But he hadn't. The book that would make me immortal was exactly where I left it. The twigs were still on top. God hadn't even looked at it!

I picked up the pages, rolled them into a tube and raised it to my mouth. "You're not very polite!" I yelled at the sky.

\* \* \*

"Mrs. Utley says angels come get you when you die." My mother was straightening the bed sheet around me and my favorite birthday present, a Storybook doll with black hair and a long plaid taffeta skirt. "Do they come down the chimney?"

"I think they come through the window," she said. "Like Peter Pan."

"Can you close the window?"

My mother hesitated. She looked like she was going to say something. She closed the window and sat down on the edge of my bed.

"Does God ever forget promises you make?" I asked.

"No," she said softly. She stroked my arm. Little light-feather strokes. "But sometimes he overlooks them."

Overlooks? Like the time my mother caught me trying to feed peanut butter to the dog. "I'll overlook it this one time," she said. Or when the Vandervelt brothers got their model plane stuck on our roof for the fifth time in one week and my father said he was going to throttle them, but my mother said just overlook it.

I hugged my mother so tight she started to cough. The best

thing I could ever wish for in my whole life had happened. The angels weren't coming for me! I wasn't going to die and get put in a box. God, in his immortal, eternal, infinite wisdom, had overlooked me!

It was several days before the thorny thought occurred that maybe God hadn't overlooked me after all. Maybe he just plain forgot. People were always forgetting people's birthdays. And if that was the case, he could remember any day now. Each minute could be my last!

I developed a small tic. I closed my window every night to make it harder for the angels to get in. I became obsessed with figuring out what was absolutely true and what wasn't. In my family the line was fine indeed. At age seven, I was becoming officially neurotic. My parents didn't seem to notice.

# Sign from the Ceiling

My best friend in third grade was Patsy Wentworth. We shared toys, clothes and a crush on the same boy. One Saturday Patsy's mother said I could spend the night and go with them to Mass the next morning if I promised to be very quiet and polite. I was quiet and polite by nature, but Mrs. Wentworth seemed to think an uncharacteristic raucousness might overtake me at this event called Mass.

Patsy was the only Catholic girl I knew and Rachael Adler was the only Jew. Having given up trying to understand the answers I got from my parents and Mrs. Utley, I turned to them with my deep theological questions. Like how does your soul get out of your body when you die?

Rachael wasn't sure, but Patsy knew exactly how it happened. "Catholic souls get out through their belly button," she said, "because that's how the angel made Mary pregnant."

I was impressed by her unwavering certainty. To wit: I wore a Band-aid over my belly button for two years lest my soul get out or a baby get in.

"What's your church like?" I asked with a mouth full of Rice Krispies. It was Sunday morning and I was the only one allowed to eat before Mass because I was Methodist and according to the Wentworths, going to hell because of it.

"Just like yours," Patsy said, handing me something that looked like a doily to wear on my head and a bobby pin to hold it in place.

She was wrong, her church was not just like mine. For one thing, there was a big stone washbowl inside the front door that looked like Mrs. Bonzell's bird bath. Patsy put her hand in the water and touched her forehead. I started to do it too, but Mrs. Wentworth snatched my hand in midair and shook her head.

There were statues everywhere and trays of candles lit up like Christmas in little red and blue glasses and purple banners on the wall and a long table up front with a white lace cloth.

All we had at our church was a dinky brown stand for Reverend Nutting to lean on when he talked.

At the Wentworths' church, the ceiling was blue and pink and gold with baby angels flying around and an old man floating on a cloud. On the wall a huge bloody Jesus hung from a cross. I tried not to look.

"Who's that?" I pointed to the statue of the most beautiful lady I'd ever seen. She had stars around her head.

"Holy Mary Mother of God," Patsy said.

God had a mother? How had I missed that in Mrs. Utley's class? "God had a mother?" I said loud enough for people across the aisle and three rows down to hear.

Mrs. Wentworth put a finger over her lips and scowled a shushing scowl. Then for good measure she gave my puffed sleeve a yank and shushed me again. Before I could ask for clarification the music started, everyone stood up and a whole parade of folks walked down the aisle carrying shiny things on long poles.

Instead of plain old black like Reverend Nutting wore, the minister at Patsy's church had on a green and gold robe with a hood and sashes and a rope around his waist. Rickie and Ronnie Marconi carried tall candles. Danny Ripley swung a long chain with a silver ball on the end that looked like it was on fire. The boys wore white dresses over their clothes. Dresses! I was entranced.

Danny swished the smoky ball back and forth filling the church with a smell as sweet as my mother's Chantilly perfume.

People knelt down and stood right back up. They patted their foreheads and chests, played with beads and mumbled words I couldn't understand. Except for one. I was pretty sure I heard Mr. Wentworth say *eternal*.

The minister poured something into a silver cup. "It's wine," Patsy whispered.

"Wine!" I gasped. Mrs. Wentworth pinched my lips together and held them squeezed shut until people started to get up and walk to the front of the church.

"You stay here," she ordered. "You're not Catholic." It was something I planned to rectify immediately.

The next-to-last thing I remember seeing as I sat alone fiddling with my head-doily and waiting for the Wentworths to return, was the minister putting something in Mrs. Wentworth's mouth. The very last thing I remember was a little chunk of gold-painted plaster falling into my lap.

"Maybe it was the incense," Mr. Wentworth said as I opened my eyes. I was slumped in the corner of the pew clutching the gold nugget.

"Could have been all the kneeling," Mrs. Wentworth said. She was fanning my face with her pocketbook.

"Look what fell in my lap at Patsy's church!" I shoved my hand between the newspaper and my father's face. "Mrs. Wentworth says maybe it's a sign." Actually what she said was, "Maybe it's a sign from God," but the God word made my father blink and clear his throat over and over so I avoided using it.

"It's a sign, all right," he said. "A sign the church needs to fix their ceiling." I liked Mrs. Wentworth's version better.

"Why aren't we Catholic?" I asked.

"Because we're Methodist." That wasn't quite true. My mother was Methodist. My father hadn't set foot in a church since he was eight. Even to get married. It worried me. Once I tried to baptize him while he was asleep on the couch. He woke up damp, confused and demanding an explanation.

"What if we want to be Catholic?" I asked.

"We don't."

"What if *I* want to be Catholic?"

"You can't." This wasn't going the way I'd hoped.

"Did you know God had a mother?" I said, abandoning for the moment my plan to convert.

"Don't be silly."

What did that mean? Don't be silly, of course I knew, or don't be silly, God doesn't have a mother? I took the safe road. "What's eternal?"

"Something that goes on forever," my father said. "Rather like your questions." He smiled at his own wit and snapped the wrinkles out of the newspaper to signal I was dismissed.

I wrapped the piece of gold plaster in a Kleenex and put it under my pillow. Every night that week before I turned out the light, I checked to make sure my treasure was still there. On Saturday Mrs. Crumley washed it with the sheets.

"Please let me go," I begged Mrs. Wentworth. "I promise I won't talk and I promise I won't faint!" I was hoping another sign would fall in my lap to replace the one that disintegrated in the Maytag wringer-washer. She gave in when Patsy said if I went to Mass, maybe I'd grow up to be a *none*. No matter how unfortunate that sounded, a sign from God was worth the risk.

Mrs. Wentworth agreed I could come along, "But you are not to kneel and you must put a handkerchief over your nose when the acolyte swings the incense burner." I agreed even though I had no idea what an acolyte was.

I followed instructions about not kneeling and Mrs. Wentworth slapped her hand over my face when Danny Ripley swooshed the smoky ball around. In spite of the precautions, when the Wentworths returned from getting their wine and crackers, they found me slumped in the corner of the pew. Mrs. Wentworth said I was too high-strung for Mass and would never let me go with them again.

# Eggs and Spam

My crisis of faith began in Mrs. Burger's third-grade health class. Usually we talked about stuff like why spinach is our friend and how to suck venom out of a snake bite.

But one horrible awful day, the day that changed everything, Mrs. Burger showed us a movie called *Understanding Sexual Reproduction*. There were diagrams and words like fallopian tubes and ovaries and spermatozoa that made the girls squirm and the boys snort with laughter even though nobody knew what any of it meant. And there were pictures of squiggly things that looked like pollywogs racing to get to a blob that was somehow going to turn into a baby.

"That's not a blob," Mrs. Burger said. "It's an egg." The boys hooted and a few of them cackled and clucked. I, on the other hand, panicked. I had eaten an egg that very morning!

The instant the movie was over, I waved my hand in the air. "Do all eggs turn into babies?" I was fixated on my breakfast.

"Every egg that comes in contact with sperm."

I thought Mrs. Burger said Spam. My mother always cooked Spam with our eggs! My heart started to race. I raised my hand again. We weren't supposed to ask two questions in a row, but I had to know.

"Every single egg?"

"Yes."

I didn't even wait for the school bus. I ran all the way home. By the time I got there I was so out of breath I was wheezing and feeling faint. I dashed to my room and grabbed the jar of pollywogs I'd been collecting from the creek. My mother was in the kitchen washing Gerber's Vegetable Medley off my brother's face.

I banged the jar on the table so hard the water sloshed. My mother put the face cloth down. My brother stopped kicking. Both of them stared at me. "You told me these would turn into frogs, but I ate Spam and Mrs. Burger says now they're going to make babies inside me." I started to cry. And then I threw up.

That night my mother read me the chapter in *Children Are People Too* on how babies are made. It clarified the sperm-Spam thing, but not much else. The next day she phoned the principal and told him eight-year-olds are far too young to be seeing movies about sexual reproduction.

"This is Berkeley not Buffalo," the principal said, which was his answer to nearly every complaint a parent made.

I might have survived the whole human reproduction episode with little permanent damage, had it not been for Mrs. Utley's Sunday school class the very next week. Our lesson from the Methodist reader was entitled *Miracle of the Virgin Birth*. I knew as soon as I saw the words virgin and birth I was in deep trouble.

Mrs. Utley suggested we skip the actual reading of the lesson and just celebrate the miracle by talking about miracles in our own lives. But Marlene and Carlene would have none of it. "The Bible says Mary got pregnant through a word in her ear," Marlene said.

I started to breathe really fast. I looked at Mrs. Utley. Her face was almost as purple as her blouse. "Did the sperm go in her ear?" I croaked.

"There was no sperm," Mrs. Utley croaked back, wiping her forehead with her sleeve.

"NO sperm?" The room was spinning.

"Can't you hear?" Carlene harrumphed. "The Bible says she got pregnant with a WORD in her ear, not a SPERM in her ear."

Thanks to my mother and the chapter in *Children Are People Too*, the only thing I was absolutely clear about when it came to the baby-making process is that you have to have sperm. "You can't make spaghetti without the noodles," is how my mother put it.

"You can't make spaghetti without the noodles," I said.

"Now there's an idea," Mrs. Utley said. "Let's talk about our favorite food! Food can be a miracle too. Especially in China where the children don't have any."

# Just Follow Your Partner

Every Thursday afternoon in a rite of pre-pubescent madness called Social Dance, the fifth-grade boys at Arlington Elementary lined up along one wall of the P.E. room and the girls lined up along the opposite wall. When Miss Tinkham said, "You may now choose your partner," the boys dashed, shoved, punched and pummeled their way across the slippery floor, arriving in a panting heap at the feet of Sheila Sullivan and Annalise Jensen.

Sheila and Annalise giggled and made a big eenie-meenie-minie-mo production out of which boy got to dance with them, while the rest of the girls glared in disgust and envy.

I usually ended up with Fleming Duffield. Or rather Fleming Duffield ended up with me. Even though he was one of the fastest runners in school and could easily have been the first to reach Sheila and Annalise, he didn't like getting jostled. There was never any jostling around me.

Once a month the mothers were invited to watch this embarrassing spectacle. I begged my mother not to come. Every child begged every mother not to come. But it did no good. The first Thursday of the month at 2:15 p.m., twenty-four mothers filed into the Arlington Elementary P.E. room.

My mother sat on a metal folding chair, her white gloves draped neatly over her patent leather handbag, and for the next hour she smiled a sweet and loving smile while I died inside.

I had severe dance deficiency. What seemed natural and effortless for everyone else was nearly impossible for me. Even practicing alone in my bedroom with the door locked and the shades pulled I was stiff-legged and self-conscious. It was my most dreadful luck to be born to a mother who had won the all-city ballroom competition when she was a teenager. "Just follow your partner," she said when I bemoaned my inadequacy. "Any girl can be a good dancer if she has a good partner."

My partner was Fleming Duffield. He didn't lead, he pushed, like I was a bookcase or a small cupboard that had to be shoved about from place to place with great effort. "Rigid as ramrods," is what Miss Tinkham said every time we box-stepped past her. "Jiggle, jiggle, let those hippies wiggle!" Our mutual humiliation bonded us in an odd and pathetic sort of way.

Let me see! Make her move! My brother and sister were fighting for position in front of the living room window. Each wanted to be the first to see Fleming. It was the night of Miss Tinkham's Fifth Grade Cotillion at the Claremont Hotel. He was my escort.

"He looks handsome," my sister said as Fleming climbed out of his parents' dark green Chrysler. He was wearing the junior tuxedo his mother bought in the Wedding Department at Capwell's. He had a pink carnation pinned to his lapel. It matched his pink cummerbund and the wrist corsage nestled in a gold box from Modesta's Florist.

"Please don't let daddy answer the door!" I begged. My father was unpredictable. Any embarrassing anything could come out of his mouth.

My father opened the door and stuck out his hand. "Come in, son." So far so good. "Nice tux. You here to marry my daughter?"

To his everlasting credit, Fleming laughed.

"He's a nice boy," my mother whispered as she helped me with the wrist corsage. "I know you'll be safe with him." Sadly, that was true.

# The Kiss

For the next four years, more or less out of default, Fleming Duffield and I went together to every school dance and most of the parties. Never once did he try to kiss me. By the start of ninth grade, every girl I knew had been kissed, and Rosalind Roswell swore she'd gone all the way, but all Fleming and I had done was hold hands. I was determined to change that.

Each night for weeks I locked my bedroom door, painted my lips with a thick coat of Revlon's Fire and Ice and slathered my eyelashes with Vaseline to make them clump up and look thicker. I stuffed cotton balls in my training bra. I practiced kissing my crimson-lipped, bumpy-chested self in the bedroom mirror so I'd be prepared when The Moment came.

And it finally did. A month after we both got braces.

Fleming walked me home from the last school dance of the year. We stood on the porch. He stared at his feet. I stared at mine.

"Well, thank you for the nice time," I said finally. Fleming raised his head and focused his gaze just past my left ear.

Then, in a do-or-die move I didn't see coming, he lunged at me. I was midway through an open-mouth gasp when his front teeth crashed into mine and some horrible somehow, the wires of our braces got tangled. We pulled, we twisted, we writhed in pain and panic. "Shitshitshit!" That was Fleming. I'd never heard him swear. The porch light came on. My father opened the door to find us locked tooth to tooth.

"What the hell are you doing?" he said, trying to separate our heads by pulling on our hair. We shrieked. My mother came to the door, followed by my sister, my brother and our cocker spaniel who was barking wildly. Mr. and Mrs. Fitzpatrick next door raised their bedroom window to get a better look.

"Somebody get a flashlight," my mother said. "Can't you see they're stuck?"

"Call the fire department!" It was Mrs. Fitzpatrick shouting through a rolled-up magazine like a cheerleader through a megaphone. Franny Fitzpatrick, who had hated me since third grade when I forgot to invite her to a slumber party, was now standing at the window with her parents.

"I can't find the flashlight," my sister said. She was back with the Coleman kerosene camping lantern and a box of kitchen matches. That was too much for Fleming.

"I ha' to urinate," he whimpered into my mouth. Everybody, including the Fitzpatricks and the dog, became very still.

"What kind of kid says urinate?" My father was looking at me. I had no idea. "Well, you're just gonna have to hold it, son."

"I'd better call Mrs. Duffield," my mother said.

I don't know if it was the prospect of peeing in his pants or having to face his mother, but Fleming let out a blood-curdling "NO!" and in one jolting jerk, yanked his braces free and ran inside to the bathroom. I was left with a mouth full of loose wires, aching teeth, and the mortification of having the worst first kiss in the history of the world witnessed by my entire family, Mr. and Mrs. Fitzpatrick, and the only girl at school who had it in for me.

"I can't go back to school," I announced through puffy lips at breakfast the next morning. "You have to send me to boarding school. Or get me a tutor. Maybe I can live with Grandma." I was sure Franny Fitzpatrick had already told half the class. My mother passed me a bowl of runny Cream of Wheat that I had to suck through a straw.

"Don't worry dear," she said. "Franny's a nice girl and she wouldn't want to embarrass you. Besides, a lot of things could happen before September." My mother was wrong about Franny, but right about a lot of things happening before September.

# A Room Full of Ferns

My father dropped his bombshell at the Tilden Park Fourth of July picnic. The whole family was squeezed onto one scratchy army blanket spread out under a eucalyptus tree. The ground was covered with hard pointy eucalyptus caps that poked our bottoms. "Isn't this fun?" my mother bubbled as she passed around tuna sandwiches, carrot sticks and deviled eggs. It wasn't fun, but we pretended.

We were well into our sandwiches when my father cleared his throat. The bombshell bounced a few times before it exploded.

"The theater company is merging," he said. No one knew what that meant so we kept on eating. "Things change when companies merge." I reached for another deviled egg. "Sometimes we don't have a choice." My mother looked up. She had mayonnaise on her chin.

"What are you saying?" An odd and edgy tone had replaced her chirpiness.

"Actually, it's good news." I knew from the word *actually* that whatever came next was definitely not going to be good news. My father forced a smile. "We get to move to Nevada."

There was a two, maybe three-second lapse before my gentle, sweet-tempered, soft-spoken mother morphed before our eyes into Hideous Monster Mother.

"NE-VA-DA?!?" she bellowed. Everyone at the Tilden Park Fourth of July Picnic heard her. "You expect us to move to NE-VA-DA?!?" Little flecks of tuna shot out of her mouth. Steam rose from the top of her head. Her eyeballs bulged, then narrowed to fiery-red slits.

"NOBODY, do you hear me, NOBODY in this family is moving to NE-VA-DA!" Her voice was deep and raspy. The earth shook. People around us fled in terror.

At the end of August we packed up our belongings, said goodbye to the beautiful three-storey canyon home in the Berkeley hills with a view of the Bay Bridge and moved to a boxy red-brick house in Reno with a view of other boxy red-brick houses. Instead of live oak and honeysuckle, we had sagebrush and Bermuda grass.

My sister wailed for weeks. My brother ate a thousand boxes of Cheerios. My mother stopped wearing lipstick and occasionally had more than one glass of sherry before dinner.

I, on the other hand, rejoiced. My prayers had been answered. Not one person in the entire state of Nevada had heard of me or Fleming or The Kiss.

There was only one thing about this great stroke of good fortune I hadn't considered. I'd gone to school with the same kids since kindergarten. I'd never had to make all new friends and had no idea how to go about it.

The popular girls at Reno High wore makeup and angora sweaters and went steady with boys named Bud and Biff who drove big cars with fuzzy dice hanging from the rearview mirror. Most of them belonged to a synchronized marching squad that performed at football games and parades. They whispered to each other in class, and rolled their colored ankle socks down to the tops of their white buck shoes. I had never seen rolled ankle socks or fuzzy dice and no one I knew in Berkeley had a car or would be caught dead in white bucks.

The rest of the girls were quiet and plain with names like Glenda and Ruth and Fern. I yearned to be one of the popular girls in the marching squad, but I feared I was a Fern. To make matters worse we sat alphabetically in most of the classes which put me right behind Dawn Wells. *The* Dawn Wells with long hair and batty eyelashes who drove a Thunderbird convertible and would, in a few years, become Mary Ann on *Gilligan's Island.* I didn't stand a chance.

At school I was invisible. Not so at church. Reverend Grimsley was the pastor of the church my mother had us join. "I'm sure you'll like our young people," he said to me during the official new-member home visit. "We have a very active group. You'll fit right in." I knew what that meant. A room full of Ferns.

"Who'd like to be youth minister this semester?" Reverend Grimsley asked the teen class. It was my first Sunday at the new church. I had no idea what a youth minister did, but if it meant wearing a long black robe and lighting candles, that's what I wanted. I shot my hand up.

"Don't be shy," he urged, "must be somebody else." No other hands. "Well then," he said finally, "looks like it'll have to be our newcomer."

As it turned out, the youth minister didn't wear a black robe or light candles. She gave an occasional fifteen-minute youth sermon to the congregation. To the whole town, in fact, because the nine o'clock service was broadcast live on the radio.

"What should I talk about?" I was scheduled to speak the first Sunday in October.

"Whatever's in your heart," Reverend Grimsley said. "Maybe you could talk about questions you have. We all have questions about God and the Bible."

I had so many questions about God and the Bible it would take a thousand 15-minute sermons to get them all out. "Are you sure?" I asked.

"Absolutely," he said.

And so I did. At both services and on the radio. People talked about it for months. Parents crossed the street and covered their children's eyes when they saw me coming. My mother had to stop going to church for a while.

My first and last sermon as youth minister was entitled: "Was Mary Really a Virgin and Was She White?"

# Peter Piper Picked a Peck

My sister grew up to be perky, outgoing and cheerleader cute. Her goal was to get married and have lots of babies. My father adored her. My mother adored her. Everyone adored her.

I, on the other hand, was studious, self-conscious and intense. My goal was to become an archaeologist, see the world, figure out absolute truth and write a book that would make me immortal before God remembered I should have died when I was seven.

My father tolerated me. My mother wrung her hands. Everyone else pretty much ignored me. Except, for the briefest of brief moments, Fathers Flannigan and Burnside at Saint Mary of the Desert Catholic Church. More about them in a minute.

During high school, my sister and I occupied identical knotty pine-walled basement bedrooms connected by a walk-through closet.

At night she read *True Romance* by flashlight. I read *Coming of Age in Samoa* and *Gods, Graves and Scholars*.

While my sister practiced high kicks and catchy cheers, I worked after school selling popcorn and candy at one of my father's theaters. I had the afternoon shift. Glenda Briggs worked evenings. We shared one faded, brown and yellow uniform that we switched into and out of behind the movie screen where my father stored huge sacks of already popped popcorn. I earned 67-and-a-half-cents an hour and saved every half cent of it.

By the time I was ready to graduate I had enough money put away to travel by bus with Patsy and Rachael from San Francisco to Mexico City for three months of language school. We'd been planning it for a year. Patsy and Rachael wanted to fall in love and lose their virginity. Oh yes, and learn Spanish. I, being odd to the very core, wanted to crawl on my knees, pilgrim fashion, up the steps of the cathedral built to honor the Virgin of Guadalupe that I'd read about in *National Geographic*. And possibly fall in love, lose my virginity and learn Spanish.

I'd been a closet Catholic ever since my experience with the Wentworths. I practiced genuflecting in front of the full-length mirror in my bedroom. I read *Lives of the Saints*. I wrapped a white scarf around my forehead and draped my mother's black velvet cape over my head to see what I'd look like as a nun, which I was convinced was my true calling.

"What's the matter with your daughter?" my father asked when I started crossing myself before meals. He said, *Your Daughter* like it was my name.

Every Sunday after the 11 o'clock service at Idlewild Methodist, I ran across the street to noon Mass at St. Mary of the Desert. I always sat in the same place, the aisle seat in the last pew, so I could make a quick getaway if anyone figured out I was an interloper.

One Sunday I got to church late and in my aisle seat was a big chatty woman with wild red hair. I squeezed in front of her and immediately got hemmed in by three of her big, chatty, red-haired children who entered from the other end of the row.

"Peace of God," the woman said.

"Peace of God," I answered. That much I had down pat. I felt smugly genuine.

I had figured out a system so it would look like I knew what I was saying when it came time to recite Catholic stuff. I moved my lips soundlessly, maintaining what I hoped was a pious expression, as I mouthed, "Peter Piper picked a peck (pause) of pickled (pause) peppers..."

"Are you from Yugoslavia, dear?" the wild-haired woman asked after I Peter-Pipered the Apostle's Creed.

"Yes," I said.

Right before communion, I usually scooted out the side door and ran home to lunch. But this time the woman and her children all stood up at once which meant I had to stand too because they couldn't get around me. Horror of horrors, before I knew it I was wedged panicky and frantic between the woman and her biggest, chattiest son in the communion line!

My heart raced. My mind raced. I imagined the word *Methodist* starting to appear in blood on my forehead. I had read about the Inquisition. I knew what they did to infidels.

As we inched closer to the front of the church, I realized I couldn't even fake it. People said something when the priest gave them the wafer and wine, and I didn't know what it was. I strained with all my might to catch the phrase. It was no use.

My face grew hot. I willed myself to faint. It didn't work. There was no escaping. I was doomed to burn in Catholic hell.

And then it was my turn. I stood in front of the priests, sweat pouring down my cheeks. "Body of Christ," Father Flannigan said and handed me a wafer. The music stopped. Time slowed. I pictured Joan of Arc lashed to the pyre as flames licked her skirt. Hysteria-driven laughter bubbled deep in my throat threatening to erupt any second. *Say something!* Father Flannigan raised his eyebrows. *Say anything!*

"Holy Mary Mother of God!" I blurted, startling myself and the priest. I heard snickers.

"Blood of Christ," Father Burnside said handing me the chalice. I raised it to my lips.

"Peter Piper picked a peck. . ."

"She's from Yugoslavia," the wild-haired woman whispered.

# Hola y Adiós

As glorious as St. Mary of the Desert was, it was nothing compared to the churches in Mexico with their massive silver altars, enormous crucifixes, and plaster saints surrounded by flowers and hundreds of little white candles.

Some of the churches had waxy bodies lying in glass coffins that I hoped with all my heart were, in fact, wax. Others had walls of discarded crutches, canes and casts along with notes of thanks from the formerly disabled.

Outside, women in embroidered blouses sold religious medals, t-shirts, candles, and glow-in-the-dark statues depicting the Virgin of Guadalupe. Story was, the Virgin filled the apron of an Indian named Diego with an imprint of her own image, and told him to tell the bishop to build her a great big fancy church.

My 17-year-old Catholic-wannabe self was giddy with delight over the magic and mystery of the story. I chose to ignore the oddly anachronistic apron-wearing Indian and the Virgin's demand for a cathedral.

Patsy helped me buy a black lace mantilla, blue plastic rosary beads and a dozen medals of various saints that I strung together on a silver chain. She thought the number of medals might be excessive, but I insisted. I wanted to fit in when I went to Mass.

In order to do that, however, I had to know the secret phrase Catholics say when the priest hands them the communion wafer. I pleaded with Patsy to tell me.

"What secret phrase?" Obviously she'd been warned not to divulge it.

"You know, when you get the wafer and the wine."

"Amen," she said.

"Amen?" I groaned. "Never Holy Mary Mother of God?"

"Never."

It took only a few days in Mexico for me to decide that more than anything I wanted to be a Mexican Catholic.

The fact that my green-eyed blondness and inability to speak Spanish hinted at another heritage didn't occur. I was home. These were my people.

I wanted to marry a Mexican man, have Mexican babies, cook Mexican food and go to Mass three times a day. It was my destiny.

Then I met Arturo. He was dark and dashing, a second-year medical student from Cuernavaca. He spoke English and danced like a dream. Even I could follow him. For a few weeks it was lovely. And then it wasn't.

"You must let the hair on your legs grow long," he said. "We Latin men find it sexy."

"You must stay home while I go to the bullfights with my mistress Begonia," he said. "We Latin men must have our freedom."

"You must abandon the idea of university," he said. "We Latin men do not want our women so educated."

"You must go fly a kite," I said. "We American women think you're full of crap."

Thus, as quickly as it began, ended my dream of Mexican men, Mexican babies, Mexican food and Mass three times a day under the beneficent gaze of plaster saints and the blue-robed Virgin of Guadalupe.

Patsy, Rachael and I returned home at the end of summer, our virginity intact. In September we started college.

# What Will the Neighbors Say?

I dashed across campus holding my umbrella in front of me as a shield against the wind and rain. All of a sudden thud, splat, and something that sounded like *argooshkaramba* as the metal tip of my umbrella struck the midsection of a short bald man with bulging eyes.

"You injured my intestines!" He had an accent and a twitch. His books and papers, wet and getting wetter, lay strewn on the ground.

"Sorry!" I said, picking up soggy pages of what looked like chemistry notes. I stuffed them into his hand as the campanile bells rang the hour. "I'm so sorry," I said again. "I really have to run."

He was waiting on the steps of Dwinelle Hall when I got out of class. "My name is Mustafa," he said. "You must pay for your carelessness by buying me coffee."

And that's how it began. The rest of my life, I mean. I, of course, thought I was just going to coffee.

We walked to the Mediterranean Café on Telegraph Avenue where rumple-haired students smoked Viceroys and talked about existentialism. Mustafa ordered two espressos in tiny cups. I had never tasted an espresso. After the first sip, I reached for the sugar.

"I'm from Egypt," he said, "near Alexandria." I'd been fascinated by Egypt ever since I read God, Graves and Scholars and now here I was sitting next to an Egyptian! Life couldn't get much better.

"Do you know Alexandria?" he asked. I shook my head. I knew about the Greeks and the ancient library and Ptolemy II, but that was probably not what he meant.

He downed his coffee in one gulp and reached for my hand which was still holding the sugar spoon. "Then you must come to my apartment. I will show you pictures."

I was eager to see pictures of Alexandria, even if it meant going to the apartment of a twitchy Arab with bulging eyes I'd known for fifteen minutes. And I might have if it weren't for my mother.

"Remember," she said just before I boarded the train for Berkeley, "a young man will use any excuse to get you to his room, but You Must Not Go."

"Mom!" I looked around the platform to see how many people had overheard.

"Once you've been deflowered, you can never again be. . ." my mother searched the clouds for the right and perfect word. Mercifully, the conductor blew his whistle. I gave her a hug and heaved my suitcases onto the train. "Flowered!" she yelled after me. "You can never again be flowered!"

"I have a class," I told Mustafa and immediately remembered that a minute earlier I'd said I was done for the day. My cheeks felt like they were going to spontaneously combust.

"Ahhhhhh," he said, shielding his eyes from the glow, "when Egyptian women blush it proves they are virtuous."

I was not virtuous, just paralyzed by parental programming and my father's obsession with maintaining the good opinion of insignificant others. "What will people think?" was his response to my every childhood misdeed from losing my lunch money to forgetting to feed the cat. "What will the neighbors say?" was reserved for public horrors like throwing up on the sidewalk.

I was reared on aphorisms. The scariest, most brain-numbing, fun-shattering, sexually stifling of all was issued forth at least once a week in the sternest of stern tones from the day I exited the womb. It was responsible for most of my fears and all my inhibitions: "Never, EVER say or do anything you wouldn't want to see on the front page of the newspaper."

That, combined with the implicit family commandment: Thou shalt not, under any circumstance, express thy true feelings, had created in me a hyperactive internal censor and a mind that could reason, analyze and observe but only rarely identify feelings. I had grown up in Berkeley with the Cal campus as backdrop and playground. Sweet, safe, quiet days.

But this was different. These were the days of Mario Savio and the Free Speech Movement. Of riots and sit-ins filmed daily by camera crews from every major network. Of civil rights demonstrations spurred on by a gorgeous young Joan Baez singing We Shall Overcome on the steps of Sproul Hall. Dark, dangerous days on a campus full of anarchists and pot-smoking protestors shouting fuck this and fuck that. Oh how I longed to shout "fuck!" But I knew if I did it would end up on the front page of the Berkeley Daily Gazette.

Now, at 19, in the eye of a raging sociological storm that had the nation mesmerized, I was nothing more than a benumbed spectator, afraid to become involved because of what the neighbors might say. Cranky old Mrs. Bonzell who was so fat she could barely waddle to the mailbox; Mrs. Heath, the piano teacher, who slapped the back of my hand whenever I played an errant note; Phil and Phyllis Buzzy who walked around the house in their underwear with the window shades up. These were the people who ruled my life. The idea I could drop this illusory shackle had not yet occurred to me.

Mustafa kept showing up outside Dwinelle Hall. Every few days he invited me for coffee, and a couple of times we had a hamburger on the deck at Kip's. The topic of conversation was always the same. I asked him about Egypt. He asked me how much money my father made, what kind of car he drove, how much our house was worth, and if I knew how to cook, sew and type. (No, no and yes.)

When the semester ended, I took the train back to Reno. Two weeks later Mustafa showed up at our front door.

"Who is he and why is he here?" my mother whispered.

"Why are you here?" I asked. We were sitting on the front lawn under the big weeping willow tree.

He cracked his knuckles. "To see if your family is suitable."

He twisted one arm around the back of his head and cracked his neck. I cringed. "I have decided to marry you." And then he kissed me. An awkward, passionless kiss in the middle of the day in the middle of the lawn where all the neighbors could see.

In that single, absurdly ludicrous moment the possibilities for my life shifted like destinations on one of those huge reader boards in European train stations. Not because of the kiss, which was perfunctory at best, but because in that instant of stunning incongruity, the thought that occurred to me was fuck the neighbors!

* * *

A month later, based on staggering naiveté and a passionate desire to see the world, I agreed to marry Mustafa. My parents were horrified.

"You can't be serious!" my mother howled. "If you have to marry a foreigner, why can't you marry a Swede?" That might have been my preference too, but I didn't know any Swedes.

"You can't be serious!" my father barked. "He's 15 years older than you. By the time you're 45, he'll be 60." I couldn't imagine ever being 45. "Besides, what will people say?"

"I always thought you'd marry Fleming Duffield," my sister said. So did I, but Fleming Duffield turned out to have more than a passing interest in Nate Appleby.

"He bosses you around," Patsy said.

"But he's getting a Ph.D.," Rachael mused. "He'll be Doctor Bossy. Besides, what if he's the only person who ever asks her?"

That thought had occurred to me.

"Are you in love with him?" Patsy had her hands on her hips, daring me to say yes.

I'd never been in love, except maybe with James Dean, and I wasn't sure what it was supposed to feel like. Mustafa was interesting in a quirky sort of way, but it was the idea of living in Egypt that tugged at my very soul. I had yearned to see the world ever since I toddled off down Olive Street with my pink cardboard suitcase at age two years, ten months. This might be my only chance. I'd read Jane Austen—if Elizabeth Bennet could learn to love that rude Mr. Darcy, I could learn to love Mustafa. And in the meantime, life would be one long vacation!

What I didn't know was that while he was my passport to adventure, I was his passport to a Ph.D. The Egyptian government had cancelled Mustafa's scholarship and he needed someone, or someone's parents, to support him while he finished his dissertation.

# I Should Have Been a Nun

"Why do you have to get married in an Islamic Center?" My mother had dragged me into the bathroom and locked the door. "What even *is* an Islamic Center?" She was speaking in a hush so Mustafa wouldn't hear. "Sounds like some kind of cult. And why San Francisco? What's wrong with the Methodist church right here in town? You have your whole life ahead of you, why do you have to marry the first person who asks you? We don't know a thing about him. Why does he twitch like that? He could have Saint Vitus Dance for all we know." My mother didn't want answers, she wanted to go on record as having asked the questions.

"I hope you know what you're doing," my father said with his mouth full of Raisin Bran. This was my last morning at home before returning to Berkeley. He shoved another spoonful of bran flakes in his mouth. "Don't come crying back here if it doesn't work out." He picked up the newspaper and opened it to the theater page. I could hear his jaw pop as he chewed. I hated that sound.

"He doesn't mean it," my mother said and handed me a fancy box from Joseph Magnin's tied with gold and silver ribbon. Inside, wrapped in tissue, was a sleeveless white dress with a pleated skirt and a little navy jacket. "Since you won't be walking down the aisle," she sighed, "I thought you might like something functional."

I'd been cutting out pictures of wedding dresses since I was 13. I begged for a subscription to *Modern Bride* for my 16th birthday. I had my tiara and veil all picked out. And the flowers—yellow roses with sprigs of lily of the valley. Patsy would be my maid of honor and Rachael would be a bridesmaid. They would wear pale turquoise with shoes dyed to match and a string of cultured pearls.

I slipped the navy jacket on over my t-shirt. So what if I couldn't wear my dream dress with sweetheart neckline and long satin train. I'd get to live in Egypt! I hugged my mother. "It's perfect," I said.

Instead of the lavish rehearsal dinner at I'd envisioned, the night before our wedding Mustafa and I had a milkshake at Edy's Ice Cream Parlor. Afterwards, I walked across campus to North Gate. The air was warm and smelled like cut grass. My destination was All Souls Episcopal Church on Cedar Street, as close to Catholic as we had in the neighborhood. The sanctuary was open and empty. I slid into a pew.

"I'm getting married tomorrow," I whispered to the empty space. "To a Moslem." Maybe God already knew that. I wasn't clear about the omniscient part. "Moslems believe in God so it's all the same, right?" My mother said it most definitely was not all the same, but she'd been wrong before and I wanted her to be wrong this time. I willed a sign to appear that some heavenly somebody had heard what I said and wished me well. Nary a candle flicker.

It was almost 7 o'clock when I looked at my watch. The sexton would be there soon to lock up. I walked to the back of the church where a painting of Mary hung on the wall in an ornate gold frame. "I would have made a great nun," I said to the sweet, solemn face, "if it weren't for the Methodist thing."

I knew that probably wasn't true. I was stubborn and vain and asked way too many questions to make a good nun. But I liked thinking about it.

I dipped my hand in the holy water, crossed myself and walked out into the red-sky sunset. If all went as planned, a year from now I'd be riding a camel.

# About the Author

Sharon Mehdi has spent most of her life not writing a book about absolute truth that will make her immortal. She feels guilty about it. But what can you do.

In the meantime she lived 16 years (off and on) in the Middle East—Egypt, Lebanon, Iraq and Kuwait; survived three wars; had four children; taught English; backpacked 500 miles across Spain; became a healer; rode a school bus filled with medical supplies from Seattle to Guatemala; fitted eyeglasses for Mayan villagers; made 18 research trips to Europe; organized an all-woman archaeological dig in France; wrote and performed a one-woman play entitled *She Never Said Her Name Was Mary*; became a clinical hypnotherapist specializing in past-life regression; wrote and directed a small film; made meals for migrant farm workers in Colorado for a year; and taught workshop participants from around the world how to heal fear.

This last she did in the shadow of the famed Gothic cathedral in Chartres, France dedicated to the Blessed Virgin. The cathedral wherein may lie the Golden Scrolls of Knowledge so filled with absolute truth they could heal this weary world of ours.

But that's a story for another day.

CPSIA information can be obtained
at www.ICGtesting.com
Printed in the USA
LVHW102110100720
660314LV00011B/404